WORLD AT WAR

Fall of Singapore

SOME MAJOR EVENTS IN WORLD WAR II

THE EUROPEAN THEATER

1939 SEPTEMBER—Germany invades Poland Great Britain, France, Australia, & New Zealand declare war on Germany; Battle of the Atlantic begins. NOVEMBER—Russia invades Finland.

1940 APRIL—Germany invades Denmark & Norway. MAY—Germany invades Belgium, Luxembourg, & The Netherlands; British forces retreat to Dunkirk and escape to England. JUNE—Italy declares war on Britain & France; France surrenders to Germany. JULY—Battle of Britain begins. SEPTEMBER—Italy invades Egypt; Germany, Italy, & Japan form the Axis countries. OCTOBER—Italy invades Greece. NOVEMBER—Battle of Britain over. DECEMBER—Britain attacks Italy in North Africa.

1941 JANUARY—Allies take Tobruk. FEBRUARY—Rommel arrives at Tripoli. APRIL—Germany invades Greece & Yugoslavia. JUNE—Allies are in Syria; Germany invades Russia. JULY—Russia joins Allies. AUGUST—Germans capture Kiev. OCTOBER—Germany reaches Moscow. DECEMBER—Germans retreat from Moscow; Japan attacks Pearl Harbor; United States enters war against Axis nations.

1942 MAY—first British bomber attack on Cologne. JUNE—Germans take Tobruk. SEPTEMBER—Battle of Stalingrad begins. OCTOBER—Battle of El Alamein begins. NOVEMBER—Allies recapture Tobruk; Russians counterattack at Stalingrad.

1943 JANUARY—Allies take Tripoli. FEBRUARY—German troops at Stalingrad surrender. APRIL—revolt of Warsaw Ghetto Jews begins. MAY—German and Italian resistance in North Africa is over; their troops surrender in Tunisia; Warsaw Ghetto revolt is put down by Germany. JULY—allies invade Sicily; Mussolini put in prison. SEPTEMBER—Allies land in Italy; Italians surrender; Germans occupy Rome; Mussolini rescued by Germany. OCTOBER—Allies capture Naples; Italy declares war on Germany. NOVEMBER—Russians recapture Kiev.

1944 JANUARY—Allies land at Anzio. JUNE—Rome falls to Allies; Allies land in Normandy (D-Day). JULY—assassination attempt on Hitler fails. AUGUST—Allies land in southern France. SEPTEMBER—Brussels freed. OCTOBER—Athens liberated. DECEMBER—Battle of the Bulge.

1945 JANUARY—Russians free Warsaw. FEBRUARY—Dresden bombed. APRIL—Americans take Belsen and Buchenwald concentration camps; Russians free Vienna; Russians take over Berlin; Mussolini killed; Hitler commits suicide. MAY—Germany surrenders; Goering captured.

THE PACIFIC THEATER

1940 SEPTEMBER—Japan joins Axis nations Germany & Italy.

1941 APRIL—Russia & Japan sign neutrality pact. DECEMBER—Japanese launch attacks against Pearl Harbor, Hong Kong, the Philippines, & Malaya; United States and Allied nations declare war on Japan; China declares war on Japan, Germany, & Italy; Japan takes over Guam. Wake Island, & Hong Kong; Japan attacks Burma.

1942 JANUARY—Japan takes over Manila; Japan invades Dutch East Indies. FEBRUARY—Japan takes over Singapore; Battle of the Java Sea. APRIL—Japanese overrun Bataan. MAY—Japan takes Mandalay; Allied forces in Philippines surrender to Japan; Japan takes Corregidor; Battle of the Coral Sea. JUNE—Battle of Midway; Japan occupies Aleutian Islands. AUGUST—United States invades Guadalcanal in the Solomon Islands.

1943 FEBRUARY—Guadalcanal taken by U.S. Marines. MARCH—Japanese begin to retreat in China. APRIL—Yamamoto shot down by U.S. Air Force. MAY—U.S. troops take Aleutian Islands back from Japan. JUNE—Allied troops land in New Guinea. NOVEMBER—U.S. Marines invade Bougainville & Tarawa.

1944 FEBRUARY—Truk liberated. JUNE—Saipan attacked by United States. JULY—battle for Guam begins. OCTOBER—U.S. troops invade Philippines; Battle of Leyte Gulf won by Allies.

1945 JANUARY—Luzon taken; Burma Road won back. MARCH—Iwo Jima freed. APRIL—Okinawa attacked by U.S. troops; President Franklin Roosevelt dies; Harry S. Truman becomes president. JUNE—United States takes Okinawa. AUGUST—atomic bomb dropped on Hiroshima; Russia declares war on Japan; atomic bomb dropped on Nagasaki. SEPTEMBER—Japan surrenders.

WORLD AT WAR

Fall of Singapore

By R. Conrad Stein

Consultant
    Professor Robert L. Messer, Ph.D.
    Department of History
    University of Illinois at Chicago Circle

CP CHILDRENS PRESS, CHICAGO

The blazing battleship *West Virginia* after the
Japanese attacked Pearl Harbor on December 7, 1941.

FRONTISPIECE:
The palm-lined shore of the
island of Singapore.

Library of Congress Cataloging in Publication Data

Stein, R. Conrad.
  Fall of Singapore.

  (World at war)
  Includes index.
  Summary: Details the bloody defeat of the
supposedly impregnable Singapore by the Japanese in
1942, an event which signaled the end of European
colonial empires in the Far East.
  1. World War, 1939–1945—Singapore—Juvenile
literature.   2. Singapore—Siege, 1942—Juvenile
literature.   3. World War, 1939–1945—Campaigns—
Malay Peninsula—Juvenile literature.   4. Malay
Peninsula—History—Juvenile literature.
[1. Singapore—Siege, 1942.   2. World War,
1939–1945—Campaigns—Malay Peninsula]
I. Title.   II. Series.
D767.55.S85   1982   940.54'25   82-9416
ISBN 0-516-04796-5   AACR2

PICTURE CREDITS:

WIDE WORLD PHOTOS: Cover, pages 6,
13, 14 (bottom), 15, 21, 23, 24, 27, 28
(top), 31, 33, 35 (top), 36 (top), 39, 40
(bottom), 42, 43, 44
UPI: Pages 4, 9, 14 (top), 18, 22,
28 (bottom), 35 (bottom), 36 (bottom),
40 (top)
COLOUR LIBRARY INTERNATIONAL:
Page 46
LEN MEENTS (map): Page 10

COVER PHOTO: A Malayan mother
and daughter grieve over the death of
another child, killed by bomb fragments
during one of the last Japanese
bombing raids before the city of
Singapore fell.

PROJECT EDITOR
Joan Downing
CREATIVE DIRECTOR
Margrit Fiddle

In the winter of 1941, the British people who lived in Singapore gave many parties. These men and women partied to take their minds off the dangers that surrounded them. At home, England was locked in a desperate war with Germany. In the Pacific, Japan was on the brink of war with the Western Allies. The British citizens of Singapore lived in fear that they soon would have to fight two powerful enemies on opposite sides of the world.

Many of the partygoers were still out at two in the morning—Singapore time—on December 8, 1941. Then some frightening news crackled over the radio. The announcer said an American base called Pearl Harbor, in Hawaii, was under attack by Japanese airplanes. The British men and women wondered when the Japanese would strike Singapore, too. They did not have to wait long for an answer. Only two hours after the first bombs fell on Pearl Harbor, Japanese airplanes screamed toward Singapore.

Just as they did to the United States, the Japanese declared war against Great Britain by launching a surprise attack.

Bombs whistled out of the night sky. The thunder of explosions rocked the city. Japanese pilots had a perfect target. Below them the streetlights of Singapore glowed brightly. Frantic city officials tried to turn the lights off. But the man who had the key to the master switch was out having a bite to eat. So the streetlights of Singapore burned at full power during the entire air raid.

Sixty-three people were killed and twice that number were injured during that first air raid. Almost all of the casualties were civilians. This air raid, however, was only the beginning of a long ordeal the civilians would suffer during the battle of Singapore.

Singapore, before the Japanese attacked, looked peaceful except
for the concrete machine-gun pillboxes located throughout the city.

KOREA

JAPAN

CHINA

TAIWAN

SOUTHEASTERN ASIA

● HONG
KONG

BURMA

LAOS

PACIFIC OCEAN

THAILAND

VIETNAM

CAMBODIA

PHILIPPINE
ISLANDS

MALAY
PENINSULA

● *Kuala Lumpur*

SINGAPORE

SUMATRA

BORNEO

AUSTRALIA

Singapore is an island at the tip of the Malay Peninsula. For one hundred years it had been a bastion of British power in the Far East.

Long before World War II, European countries had carved out colonies in Asia. Eventually, the Europeans lost their power in the area. But in 1941 Europeans still had control over large areas in the Pacific. Great Britain owned the biggest and richest colonies in Asia. The British ruled those colonies from their island headquarters at Singapore.

The island of Singapore is twenty-six miles long and fourteen miles wide. Busy Singapore City, on the tip of the island, had a population of about two million in 1941. The name Singapore means "City of the Lion." The lion is king of the jungle. Like a lion, the island of Singapore seemed too strong to be conquered by any foe.

In the opening moments of the war, Japan had two major objectives. One was to destroy the American fleet at Pearl Harbor. The other was to drive the British out of the Pacific by taking Singapore. In one shocking morning, the Japanese accomplished their goal at Pearl Harbor. Five American battleships—the heart of the United States Pacific fleet—lay at the bottom of the harbor. At the same time bombs were raining down on Pearl Harbor, Japanese troops were landing in northern Malaya. Their orders were to march south and invade Singapore.

Despite the first air raid, most Englishmen thought the Japanese would not be able to conquer their stronghold at Singapore. The island seemed to be safe from invasion either by land or by sea.

In order to invade Singapore by land, an enemy would have to march down the forbidding Malay Peninsula. Malaya is covered

One of Singapore's huge, long-range coastal guns fires a test shot.

with thick jungle—a maze of vines and trees growing on beds of swamp and quicksand. Beyond the jungle, the island of Singapore was separated from the tip of the peninsula by a channel about the width of three football fields. That channel shielded the island like the moats that once surrounded ancient castles.

Only a very foolish enemy would dare attack Singapore from the sea. Protecting the island on the seaward side were rows and rows of long-range guns that could blast any invading fleet out of the water.

Bolstering the island's defenses were the battle cruiser *Repulse* and the battleship *Prince of Wales*. The two mighty warships had arrived one week before the Japanese attack. They had been sent to Singapore by British Prime Minister Winston Churchill. The *Repulse* was a veteran of World War I. The *Prince of Wales* was spanking new and the pride of the British fleet.

The battleship
Prince of Wales

The battle
cruiser
Repulse

General Tomoyuki Yamashita, commander of the Japanese infantry in Malaya.

So most Englishmen believed Singapore was an impregnable fortress nestled behind an impassable jungle. In addition, the island was defended by two of the most powerful battleships in the world.

But hundreds of miles to the north, Japanese soldiers poured out of landing ships onto jungle beaches. They were commanded by a hard-driving general named Yamashita. He believed his tough infantrymen could march through the "impassable" jungle and attack Singapore from the land.

Reports of Japanese landings in northern Malaya reached British naval headquarters in Singapore. The *Repulse, Prince of Wales,* and four destroyers were sent to find and sink the invading ships. Commanding the flotilla was Admiral Sir Tom Phillips. Because he was only five feet, four inches tall, Phillips was known in the British fleet as "Tom Thumb" Phillips.

Phillips believed his ships could outfight anything the Japanese had at sea. But he knew he would be operating well within the range of Japanese air bases in Indochina. The Admiral wanted fighter cover on this mission.

Shortly after he weighed anchor, an aide handed Phillips a radiogram. It read: REGRET FIGHTER PROTECTION IMPOSSIBLE.

Phillips shrugged his shoulders and said to his staff, "Well, we must get on without it."

The Admiral knew he was being denied fighter cover because Japanese soldiers had already captured a key airfield in northern

Malaya. Certainly he did not know that as he steamed northward a periscope popped out of the water on his starboard side. That periscope belonged to the Japanese submarine *I-58*. The *I-58* radioed Japanese airfields giving them the position of the British ships. For Japan, the sub's chance sighting of the British flotilla was an incredibly lucky break.

At 11:00 A.M. on the third day of the war, a lookout on board the *Repulse* spotted what appeared to be a dot in the sky. Suddenly more dots broke out of the clouds. "Aircraft!" shouted the lookout. "Aircraft off the port side."

A siren screamed over the loudspeakers. An excited voice announced, "Enemy aircraft approaching. Action stations!"

Nine Japanese bombers in single file roared toward the two battleships and their destroyer escorts. Antiaircraft guns opened fire. Shells bursting near the attacking planes left black puffs of smoke. Orange tracer bullets streamed

The *Repulse* fires its big guns.

into the sky. Still the Japanese pilots kept their planes boring straight toward the two huge battleships.

American newsman Cecil Brown stood on the deck of the *Repulse* as the bombers approached. As if he were hypnotized, Brown watched one plane release its two bombs. The bombs fell silently toward him, getting larger and larger. Suddenly Brown felt the deck under his feet lurch violently into the air. The *Repulse* had been hit.

Seconds after the bomber attack, more planes skimmed over the water. One by one they dropped their torpedoes. The torpedoes splashed into the choppy water and darted toward their targets. Two torpedoes struck the stern of the *Prince of Wales*. This was the ship's most vulnerable spot. With a mighty roar, the torpedoes exploded under the ship. The explosions shattered the rudder. The *Prince of Wales* sent this desperate message: WE HAVE LOST CONTROL OF OUR SHIP.

A destroyer captain read the message. Sadly he shook his head, knowing the great ship was doomed. In battle a ship must be able to maneuver. Without maneuverability, the huge *Prince of Wales* drifted helplessly.

New waves of Japanese bombers now zoomed out of the clouds. Eighty-five airplanes swarmed over the two ships like angry bees. More bombs fell. The *Repulse* and the *Prince of Wales* seemed to disappear under geysers of water and great clouds of billowing smoke.

Finally the Japanese airplanes sped away. Behind them the two British capital ships were in smoking ruins.

The *Prince of Wales* listed hard to port. Aboard her stood her captain, John Leach, and Admiral "Tom Thumb" Phillips. Leach ordered his men to abandon ship. As the crew lowered lifeboats and climbed over the side, Leach called out, "Good-bye. Thank you. God bless you." Those were his last words. The *Prince of Wales* keeled over and sank. Captain Leach and Admiral "Tom Thumb" Phillips went with the great ship to the bottom.

An hour before the *Prince of Wales* slipped under the water, the veteran ship *Repulse* also sank. Her captain, too, had tried to go "down with the ship" in naval tradition. But a group of his officers lifted their captain out of the command room and carried him to a lifeboat.

The sinking of the *Repulse* and the *Prince of Wales* was a shocking defeat for the British Navy.

Aerial view of the Japanese attack on the
Prince of Wales (right) and the *Repulse* (left).

More than eight hundred seamen were killed
during the battle. Only four attacking airplanes
were shot down.

Two thousand British seamen from the *Prince
of Wales* and the *Repulse* were rescued by
destroyers. The rescue operation was successful
because the Japanese airplanes chose not to
attack the destroyers or the survivors. Early in
the war, both sides honored traditional rules of
warfare and permitted the rescue of helpless
men. This chivalry did not last, however. Later
in the war, helpless soldiers and sailors often
were attacked.

Prime Minister
Winston Churchill

In London, Prime Minister Winston Churchill was alone in his bedroom when told of the loss of the two great ships and the hundreds of seamen. "I was thankful to be alone," Churchill later wrote. "In all the war I never received a more direct shock. As I turned over and twisted in bed, the full horror of the news sank in upon me."

With the sinking of the two British warships, Japan had won the naval battle of Singapore. Now their fighting ships could shell the land in support of their troops. And their merchant ships could supply their army.

The Lockheed Hudson aircraft used by the British
in Malaya (above) were out of date even in 1941.

On the ground, Japanese troops had landed at
three fishing ports on the Malay Peninsula. They
met resistance only at the port of Kota Bharu,
about four hundred miles north of Singapore.
There the British had an airfield and a brigade
of infantry. The battle for this tiny fishing port
was the first ground combat between British and
Japanese forces in World War II.

During the opening moments of the invasion,
British aircraft scrambled off Kota Bharu
runways to attack the landing ships. They were
old Hudson and Wildebeeste bombers—aircraft
that were out of date even by 1941 standards.
But they could still carry bombs. Bravely their
pilots flew through antiaircraft fire toward the

This British armored car patrolled a jungle road
in Malaya as soldiers took cover by the roadside.

Japanese ships. Three transport ships were hit
and sunk. But hundreds of Japanese soldiers
stormed the beaches from other ships.

Once on shore, the soldiers pressed toward the
British air base. Dug-in British infantrymen
fought back. Near the airfield, machine-gun fire
from a British pillbox pinned down a Japanese
company. Suddenly one Japanese infantryman
dashed forward and threw himself over the slit of
the pillbox. He was killed instantly, but his
death allowed his comrades to advance.

With fanatical courage the Japanese overran the British at Kota Bharu after a furious two-day battle. Now the air base was in Japanese hands, and the British had to face the splendid fighter plane called the Zero.

The Zero fighter took all of Japan's enemies by surprise. It was made of a lightweight aluminum alloy that allowed it to fly at great speed. The plane was also remarkably agile. The ancient British Wildebeeste bomber had a top speed of only 110 miles per hour. The Zero's top speed was 325 miles per hour. And it was so maneuverable that it could actually fly rings around the lumbering Wildebeeste. Newer British Spitfire fighters would have been a match for the Zero. But there were few Spitfires in the Far East. The precious Spitfires were in England fighting German bombers.

Within a week, Zero fighters shot down practically all of the British aircraft over Malaya. With control of both the sky and the sea, the Japanese Army pushed steadily down the Malay Peninsula.

Before 1941, the British knew little about the Japanese fighting man. Many British generals thought he was small, weak, and tired easily. Some Englishmen were so ignorant about the Japanese that they actually believed that the shape of their eyes would make them poor rifle shots. But the British commanders soon learned that the Japanese were superb infantrymen. They were disciplined, brave, and could march thirty miles a day with nothing to eat but a few handfuls of rice. And when locked in combat, the Japanese soldier fought with a shocking disregard for his own life.

Japan had been a warrior nation for hundreds of years. Through the generations, the young men of Japan had been told that death in battle was an honor, and defeat in battle was an unthinkable disgrace. Because of this training, drilled into him since boyhood, the Japanese soldier fought as if he had no fear of death. Soldiers who fight without fear can make a powerful army.

The Indian troops shown above were among those commanded by General Percival (left) in Malaya.

General Yamashita commanded a force of seventy thousand combat troops. All of them were committed to victory or death. The British commander, General A. E. Percival, had many more than seventy thousand men on the Malay Peninsula, and still more troops in reserve at Singapore. But Percival commanded a collection of Malay, Australian, Indian, and British troops. And the 37,000 Indian troops had not been adequately trained.

These members of a Hindu Indian regiment (above) and a Malayan regiment (below) helped defend the Malay Peninsula against the invading Japanese.

So although Percival had more men, he still did not have an advantage. And his soldiers definitely did not fight with the same do-or-die determination of Yamashita's men.

Most of the battles fought in Malaya raged on the few muddy roads that cut through the jungle. Leading the Japanese advance were rumbling tanks. Nowhere in Malaya did the British have a tank. Years earlier, British generals had determined that tanks would be useless in the jungle. But no one told Yamashita that. His tanks and infantry teams won battle after battle on the jungle roads. Infantrymen ran alongside the tanks or rode on top of them while attacking British positions. Tanks were especially effective against Indian troops. Many Indian soldiers came from primitive regions. They never even dreamed such things as tanks existed. Those Indian soldiers dropped their weapons and ran when they saw the metal monsters.

The Japanese also used bicycles to race down Malaya roads. Pedaling furiously, Japanese infantrymen often outdistanced their own trucks on the jungle roads. Desperately the British tried to halt the advance by blowing up bridges. But a destroyed bridge could not stop Japanese soldiers on bicycles. Holding their bicycles over their heads, the Japanese simply waded across the river.

Japanese soldiers also proved they could move over jungle-covered terrain where there were no roads at all. By careful scouting, they discovered trails known only to local hunters and trappers. Sometimes they used fallen trees to build crude rafts. Then they paddled or poled their way through swamp waterways.

For months before the Malaya operation, General Yamashita's men had practiced jungle warfare in Indochina. Now that training was paying off. To the Japanese, the jungle was almost a second home.

Members of this Hindu Indian regiment slog through the ever-present Malaya mud.

The British, on the other hand, hated and feared the jungle. The sweltering heat drained their strength. Mosquitoes bit them and bloodsucking leeches covered their bodies. The slimy leeches drove some men insane. Because the British ate more food than the Japanese, they had to carry heavier packs. Those heavy packs made the men bog down in the ever-present Malaya mud.

As New Year's Day, 1942, approached, the British forces sloshed backward through the swamps while the army of Japan rolled south.

Even though Singapore was a party-loving city, there were few celebrations that New Year's Eve. The Japanese were too close for anyone to want to celebrate. In less than a month they had driven two hundred miles down the Malay Peninsula. Another two hundred miles and they would be at the channel that separated Singapore from the mainland.

Hard-driving General Yamashita was the force behind the Japanese advance. He was a heavy man with a bull neck and a thick head. His troops admired his intelligence, but feared his temper. Often he cursed and kicked his men to make them move faster. Yamashita had been schooled in Japanese war colleges that emphasized offense. His strategy was to attack, attack, and attack again. On the front, the general seemed to be everywhere at the same time. He rode tanks, trucks, and bicycles. Where no roads existed he hurried down jungle paths, walking faster than most men could run.

Because of his action during this battle, Allied commanders nicknamed Yamashita the "Tiger of Malaya."

British General Percival believed in a strong defense. He was disappointed that his men were being outfought, but he was willing to give up ground in the Malay Peninsula. Percival believed he could stop the Japanese at the channel between Singapore and the mainland. He also thought the fast-moving Japanese forces would soon overrun their supply lines.

Japanese tanks, halted by Australian gunfire, blaze on a jungle road in Malaya.

In London, Winston Churchill nervously followed the battle being waged on the other side of the world. Like many Englishmen, he was shocked to discover that the splendid long-range guns that defended Singapore could not be turned around to fire on the approaching Japanese. Those guns and their emplacements had taken ten years to build and had cost millions of dollars. But British planners were so certain that it was impossible to attack Singapore from the land that they did not build the guns to swivel around and point across the channel. Even so, Churchill insisted that the British forces hold Singapore. He sent a letter to Percival that ended with this strong statement: "Finally, the city of Singapore must be converted to a citadel and defended to the death. No surrender can be contemplated."

By February 1, the Japanese had reached the channel that separated Singapore from the mainland. The British forces pulled back to the

Above: Japanese troops wait on the mainland for the order to attack the island of Singapore.
Left: A machine-gun pillbox in the center of Singapore City.

island fortress and demolition men blew up the causeway connecting the island to the tip of the Malay Peninsula.

Now the stage was set for the final battle.

General Yamashita immediately took the offensive. He ordered an air raid and an artillery barrage. The bombs and shells hit civilians as

Homes in the civilian section of Singapore City
were reduced to smoldering ruins by Japanese bombs.

well as soldiers. The civilians, especially the poor people, experienced warfare at its most cruel during the bloody battle of Singapore. Whole families huddled together in wooden shacks listening to the dreadful whistle of bombs and praying they would not get blown up. The poorest Malayan people, who lived in the flimsiest houses, were the first killed.

While shells screamed overhead, General Percival wondered where Yamashita was getting his supplies. Percival thought the Japanese advance had been so fast that the troops must have overrun their supply lines. But their guns were firing as if they had tons of shells. The British general had no way of knowing that the Japanese were dangerously short of supplies—especially artillery shells. The artillery barrage was part of a bluff. Yamashita was trying to make the British believe he had ample supplies for the final push. He hoped to force Percival into a quick surrender. Because of his shortage of supplies, Yamashita feared he might lose a long battle.

At nightfall, Japanese soldiers paddled across the channel in hundreds of tiny rubber boats. The British were taken by surprise. Again, Yamashita had outguessed Percival. When the sun rose, Zero fighters roared out of the sky to bomb and machine-gun the British defenders. The British had no airplanes to send up against the Zeros.

Under constant air attack, the British fell back from their channel defenses. Soon the Japanese brought tanks over the channel on large barges. Finally they constructed a pontoon bridge, and their soldiers poured across the channel.

By February 11 half of Singapore Island was occupied by Yamashita's men. Only Singapore City, on the tip of the island, remained in British hands. Every day the city came under a savage air attack. At the height of one air raid,

American newsman Yates McDonald huddled in his hotel room and started this newspaper story:

This will probably be my last message from this crumbling fortress. . . . The sky over Singapore is black with smoke from a dozen huge fires this morning. . . . The roar and crash of cannonade and bursting bombs which are shaking my typewriter and my hands which are wet with the perspiration of fright, tell me without the need of official communique that the war which started nine weeks ago 400 miles away is now on the outskirts of this shaken bastion of empire.

Japanese bombing attacks caused dozens of fires in Singapore and left the sky over the city black with smoke.

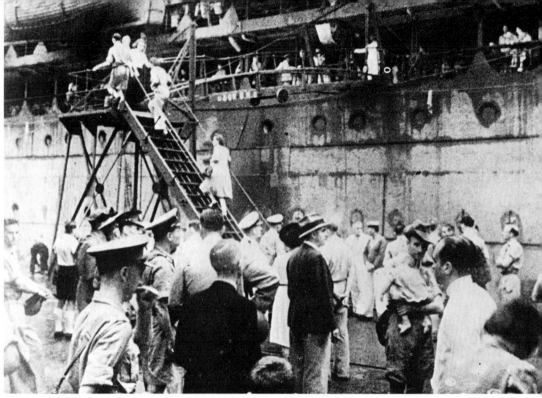

British women and children were evacuated from Singapore
shortly before the Japanese invaded the city.

The bombing and shelling caused more suffering among the Malayan civilians than it did among the soldiers of either side. In Singapore City's hospitals, the dead and dying lay in beds, under beds, and on corridor floors. Blood-spattered doctors and nurses could not begin to help the hundreds of wounded who poured to the hospitals each day. People with burns and terrible wounds lay in hospitals crying their lives away.

In his headquarters, Yamashita met with his staff. Many of his officers advised him to retreat. British forces were fighting fiercely for the remaining soil of Singapore, and the Japanese Army was running out of practically everything. Even riflemen in the field were short of bullets. His officers urged Yamashita to pull back, resupply, and attack again. Yamashita pounded a table top and screamed at his officers. He bellowed that retreat was unthinkable. Instead,

Yamashita ordered more attacks and hoped the British would not discover his desperate need of supplies.

But the British were desperate, too. Since they held the city, the thousands of wounded civilians were on their side of the island. In the middle of one battle, the city's water system broke down. With no water it became impossible to treat the masses of wounded people in the city.

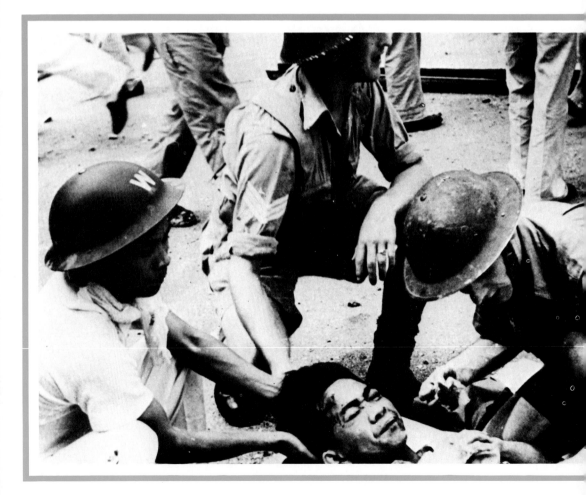

British Imperial troops aid a wounded Malay on a Singapore street.

General Percival (far right) and other British officers
on their way to meet General Yamashita and surrender to
the Japanese. The two men in the center are Japanese officers.

On February 15, 1942, General Percival made
the most difficult decision of his life. He signaled
the Japanese that he wanted to discuss
surrender. Percival and his staff met with
Yamashita and his officers in a bombed-out Ford
assembly plant on the outskirts of Singapore
City. Through an interpreter, one of Yamashita's
officers said to Percival, "Now we're coming to
the end. I compliment you on the British stand."

General Percival (right foreground, profile to camera)
and his staff at the surrender conference with General
Yamashita (seated at left, facing the camera) and his staff.

Percival just nodded. He was exhausted, and
perhaps had trouble concentrating. February 15
was a very special day for him. In England his
daughter was celebrating her twelfth birthday.

Percival asked if Japanese Army doctors
would help treat the thousands of wounded
civilians. Yamashita promised they would.
Percival sighed and signed the surrender
documents.

The battle of Singapore was over. In seventy days the Japanese had driven through what was thought to be an impassable jungle and conquered what was believed to be an impregnable fortress. Japanese forces had suffered almost 10,000 casualties. The British lost nearly as many men in the field. But some 130,000 British soldiers were taken prisoner. It was the worst defeat in England's long military history.

The fall of Singapore was also the beginning of the end of European colonial empires in the Far East. The Asian people quickly discovered the brutality of their new rulers, however, and rose up and fought them. After World War II, people in Asia and throughout the colonial world won their independence. The battle of Singapore has been called "the battle that changed the world." Certainly after what happened there the world would never be the same.

So for the British, the defeat at Singapore meant more than the loss of one battle. It meant the collapse of their empire.

Triumphant Japanese troops hoist their flag
over Singapore after the British surrender.

Index

Page numbers in boldface type indicate illustrations.

About the Author

Mr. Stein was born and grew up in Chicago. At eighteen he enlisted in the Marine Corps where he served three years. He was a sergeant at discharge. He later received a B.A. in history from the University of Illinois and an M.F.A. from the University of Guanajuato in Mexico.

Although he served in the Marines, Mr. Stein believes that wars are a dreadful waste of human life. He agrees with a statement once uttered by Benjamin Franklin: "There never was a good war or a bad peace." But wars are all too much a part of human history. Mr. Stein hopes that some day there will be no more wars to write about.